Absolute Boyfriend

Story & Art by

Yuu Watase

Act 1: The Lover Shop

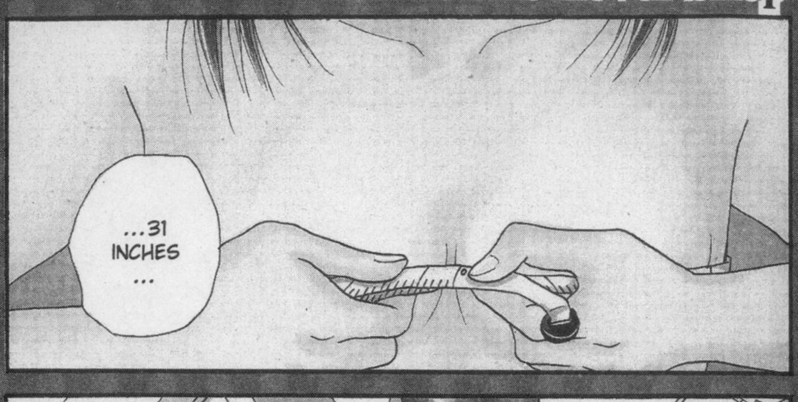

OH NO!
EEK, I GOTTA HURRY !!
MY BIG SHOW-DOWN'S THIS MORNING !!
TOKYO TRASH
WHA ...
WHOA !!
SPLAT
GASP! I FORGOT TO BRING IN THE LAUNDRY!!

WHUP
WOOSH
TWEET TWEET TWEET
...
FWAP FWAP
Yawn. GOOD MORNING, SOSHI.
IT WAS YOUR TURN TO DO THE LAUNDRY, MASAKI.
HMPH. DO I HAVE TO DO EVERY-THING AROUND HERE?

AAAH! I'M NOT GONNA MAKE IT!!

...

WUP WUP

AAGH! I HATE LIVING BY MYSELF! MOM, DAD, PLEASE COME BACK!!

TOMP TOMP TOMP

HURRY !!

CHAK

PLOP

HUH?
GACK!!
SWUP
SOSHI!? WHAT ARE YOU DOING WITH MY BRA, YOU PERVERT!?
RELAX, YOUR UNDIES AREN'T EXACTLY BUILT TO THRILL.
FLATSY-PATSY.
THWAK

IF YOU EVER CALL ME THAT AGAIN, I'LL KILL YOU!! I DON'T CARE HOW LONG WE'VE KNOWN EACH OTHER!!
CHAK
HUH? RIIKO?
Got him good.
OFF TO SCHOOL ALREADY? IT'S EARLY.
C'MON, SOSHI, THE HALL-WAY'S NO PLACE TO TAKE A NAP.
WHAT MAKES YOU THINK I'M SLEEP-ING...?
HUFF HUFF
CALM DOWN. BREATHE.
YOU'VE GOT TO DO THIS!!
GASP
G-GOOD MORNING ...
... ISHI-ZEKI!!

BA-BUMP
OH. HEY, IZAWA ...
BA-BUMP
PLEASE, CALL ME RIIKO!
BA-BUMP
SO... YOU SENT ME AN E-MAIL YESTERDAY. WHAT'S UP?
BA-
TAKE HIM ON!!
I LIKE YOU!!
WILL YOU GO OUT WITH ME!?
SORRY!
I LIKE SOME-ONE ELSE!!
WHUP

SHOT DOWN COLD!!

UM... WHAT HIT ME?
Still dazed by his speed.
OOK ...
BY THE WAY ...

WHY ARE YOU HOLDING A BRA?
Freaky.
AAAAGH...

SORRY, SEE YOU AROUND!
I GOTTA GET TO PRAC-TICE!

YOU LOSE
...WELL, PUT THE BRA AWAY!

SEIBA HIGH SCHOOL
HE DIDN'T EVEN HESITATE !!
DEJECTED
I'VE BEEN REJECTED PLENTY OF TIMES BEFORE, BUT...
...IT SUCKED. HE COULD'VE AT LEAST *PRETENDED* TO THINK ABOUT IT!
I FELL FOR HIM ON THE FIRST DAY OF SCHOOL.
IN THE MONTH SINCE, I'VE REALLY TRIED TO BE FRIENDS WITH HIM.
SOME-TIMES HE'D EVEN TALK TO ME.

*A Japanese pop singer

CUTE!? YOU'VE ONLY KNOWN HIM SINCE JUNIOR HIGH.
BACK IN GRADE SCHOOL, HE WAS A TOTAL WIMP. HE'D CRY IF ANYONE MADE FUN OF HIM A LITTLE.
NOW, I'M STUCK IN THE SAME CLASS WITH HIM AGAIN! ENOUGH ALREADY!
甘味処

ISHIZEKI IS A WHOLE LOT BETTER ...

WELL, CHEER UP! THERE ARE LOTS OF FISH IN THE SEA.
I'LL KEEP AN EYE OUT FOR YOU.
THANKS ...

SIGH ...

I HATE MY LIFE.
LOOK AT ALL THE HAPPY COUPLES. I WISH I HAD A BOYFRIEND TO WALK DOWN THE STREET WITH HOLDING HANDS! ♡

"SORRY. SORRY... ORRY... RY..."
"YOU'RE NICE, BUT... BUT... BUT... BUT...
Echo
WHY DO I ALWAYS GET REJECTED?

WILL I NEVER GET MARRIED?
WILL I WITHER AND GROW OLD WITHOUT EVER HAVING SEX!?

WILL I EVER HAVE A BOY-FRIEND!?

AND DIE ALL ALONE IN MY APARTMENT ?
GASP GASP
NEGA-TIVE SPIRAL
TING PONG
SLUMP

TWEETLE TOOT PELOG-LING ♪

♪ FWEEEET KA-BONG KA-BONG BAM-BAM-BAM

TAKKA TAKKA TAKKA TAKKA CHING CHING HAH!! ♪

A 32-chord ringtone

HERE IT IS! WHAT A WEIRD RING-TONE!

PE-LOG ♪

PE-LOG?

BEEP

HELLO?

HEY!

THANK HEAVENS! DON'T KNOW WHAT I'DA DONE IF I'D LOST IT!

BA-BUMP

IT'S A GUY...

UM... OH, ANYWAY, THANKS FOR PICKING IT UP!
HE HAS A KANSAI* ACCENT.
I GOTTA THANK YOU PROPERLY! WILL YOU MEET ME?
HUH?

*Japan's Kansai region has a distinctive dialect. See the author's commentary on p. 109 for more on this.

IT'S A PUBLIC PLACE.
AND HE SOUNDED YOUNG.
CAFE
HEY! OVER HERE!
WOW! WHAT A CUTIE PIE.
IT'S MY LUCKY DAY! ♬
BLINK
WHAT'S WITH THE OUTFIT!?
WELL, HAVE A SEAT!

IS HE INTO COS-PLAY?
Kinda cute, though.
HERE'S YOUR PHONE. UM...
THANK YOU!
HUH? OH NO, I'M JUST A REGULAR WHITE-COLLAR WORKER!
AS YOU CAN SEE.
I CAN'T!
WOULD YOU LIKE SOMETHING? OH, MISS! MENU PLEASE!
YOU SAVED ME. I NEED THIS FOR MY JOB!
YOUR JOB... WITH THE CIRCUS?
WELL, I'M IN SALES.
ANYTHING YOU WANT FROM KRONOS HEAVEN, AT A BIG DISCOUNT!!
NOW, YOU DEFINITELY DESERVE A REWARD!
HUH?
Kronos Heaven
OH... SO HE REALLY IS A SALES-MAN!!

Hi! Watase here! Welcome to my new title! Ugh, I have a headache. Maybe the summer heat is getting to me. Summer 2003 was weird. Oh well, I had so much work that I hardly ever went out. And when I did go out, it was work-related. Anyway...

About *Absolute Boyfriend*. The idea first came to me in the summer of 2002. *Alice 19th* was finishing up, so I was trying to come up with ideas for my next title. Even before that, I had this vision in my head—a naked guy tumbling out of a box. Weird, huh? I couldn't find a place for it when I first thought of the idea, so I did nothing with it and forgot about it. But it kept popping into my head. Normally, I'd just laugh it off as the wild fantasies of a single woman (ouch!), but I'm a manga artist. I knew I could find some place for it in my work! So, in about ten minutes, I came up with a bunch of ideas for characters and settings, and decided that it would be worth working on.

When I start on a new title, I draw rough sketches and jot notes in a sketchbook to show my editor. I had no trouble coming up with a distinctive look for this story. In fact, I was really on a roll. Most of the characters haven't changed since my initial drafts--I think only Soshi got significantly revised. The first version of him that I did was okay, but it didn't feel quite right, and I debated what to do right up to the last minute. My friend happened to be staying over, and I saw that she liked guys with glasses, so I decided to put glasses on Soshi!

OKAY, I WANT A *BOY-FRIEND*!!
HE'S SO PUSHY!
RIGHT NOW, THAT'S ALL I WANT!!

HERE'S MY CARD.
WUP
THIS CD-ROM WILL TAKE YOU TO OUR WEBSITE.
BUT THE SITE HAS TO REMAIN AN ABSOLUTE SECRET, OKAY?
TMP
TMP
I'LL BE IN TOUCH WITH YOU.
BYE, RIIKO.
A WEBSITE ?
DING DING
HAVE A NICE DAY!
HA
DID HE JUST SAY MY NAME !?

HEY!
HE'S GONE ... How?
KRONOS HEAVEN ...
GAKU NAMIKIRI? WHAT COUNTRY IS HE FROM?
FWIP
IT'S GOTTA BE A SCAM.
Kronos Heaven. co
ITEM SALES
GAKU NAMIKIRI
PLATINUM EDITION
I want to download

I CAN'T BELIEVE I TOLD A TOTAL STRANGER...
...THAT I WANTED A BOY-FRIEND.
DING DONG

CHAK
HEY.

WHAT DO YOU WANT? YOU JUST GET OFF WORK?
I'M COMING IN.
I'M ABOUT TO HAVE DINNER!

HEY!
SHEESH... WHAT A MESS.
IF YOU DON'T LIKE IT, THEN GO! PLEASE!

CAN'T, I'M ON DUTY.
YOUR PARENTS ASKED ME TO LOOK AFTER YOU WHILE THEY'RE AWAY.
FILE
DUST
CUT IT OUT! YOU'RE NOT PET-SITTING A RABBIT!

NO, A RABBIT CAGE WOULD BE MUCH TIDIER.

THIS IS WHY YOU CAN'T GET A GUY.

FWIP

SELF-DEFENSE !!

SOSHI... I HATE YOU.

"THIS IS WHY YOU CAN'T GET A GUY."

CHOMP CHOMP CHOMP

THAT JERK!! IF I EVER GET A BOYFRIEND, SOSHI'S A DEAD MAN!! YUM, THIS IS GOOD!!

ITEM SALES

!!

KLIK KLIK

MIGHT AS WELL TAKE A LOOK.

Kronos Heaven.co

恋 Lover 人 SHOP

COCO MILK

LOVER SHOP?

KLIK
KRONOS HEAVEN ON-LINE CATALOG. THEY'RE NEW.

WHAT THE HECK IS THIS?
ARE THEY TRAFFICKING IN HUMAN FLESH?

Lover
SHO
"WE HAVE THE IDEAL LOVER WHO EXISTS JUST FOR YOU."

LOVER FIGURE RELEASE SCHEDUL
F-FIGURES!?
Phew!
OH!

THEY'RE JUST DOLLS!
Hey...
ARE THEY SEX DOLLS!?
WHAT WAS HE THINKING, OFFERING THIS TO A MINOR!?
"MAKE HIM EVEN MORE PERFECT BY ADDING PERSONALITY OPTIONS."
"CONTRACT OF SECRECY UPON PURCHASE..."

"NIGHTLY SERIES 01" IS CURRENTLY AVAILABLE...
LET'S TAKE A LOOK.
KLIK

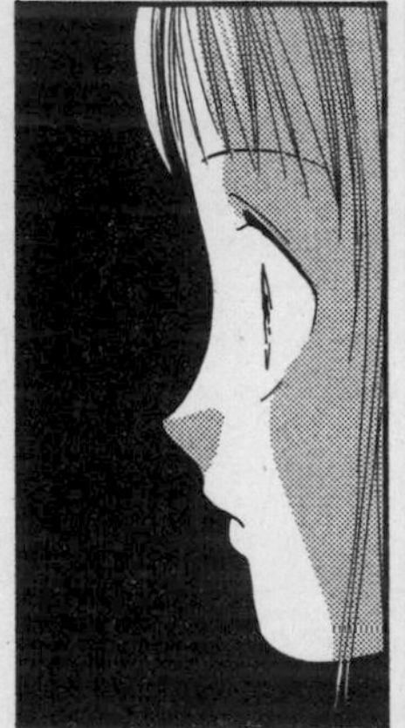

WHOA!
OH MY GOD, HE'S HOT!!
NIGHTLY
「01」
BUT STILL ...
I can't do this.
HEY!
SPECIAL PROMOTIO
3-DAY FREE TRIAL OF
TRY IT AND SEE FOR YOURSELF!
A THREE-DAY FREE TRIAL!?
I COULD TRY IT OUT...
AND RETURN IT IN THREE DAYS...
HM ...
LET'S SEE THE PERSONALITY OPTIONS ...
Not really giving it much thought.
MIGHT AS WELL INCLUDE EVERYTHING.
MEMBER REGISTRATION?
AT THE TIME ...
KLAK
KLAKETTA
KLAKETTA

...I WAS JUST CURIOUS.
BUT ...
WHAT'S IN THE BOX? A REFRIG-ERATOR?
CAUTION
Kronos Heaven
WHRR
ROOM 402.
RII-KO I-ZA-WA?
UM... YES?
PACKAGE. FOR YOU.
YOUR SIGNATURE. HERE, PLEASE.

Izawa
THANK. YOU.
GASP
YOU!
YOU!
KRONOS HEAVEN?
CAUTION
CAUTION CA
FOR REAL!? BUT I JUST ORDERED IT LAST NIGHT!
I GOTTA SEE THIS!!
RIP
RIP
OPEN UP
IT'S SO BIG.
WHY ALL THE PACKAGING?
nightly
WOBBLE
FWUMP
AAAAH!

CAUTION
HUH
...?

TMP
TMP
TMP
TMP
KLUNK
BA-
BUMP
GEEZ
...
OH...
GOD.

THIS IS TOTALLY A HUMAN BEING !!

THE FACE LOOKS SO REAL!

JUST LIKE THE PICTURE ON THE WEBSITE... AND HE'S N-NAK--

"DADDY?"

"YES, RIIKO?"

OH!

GET A GRIP.
STAGGER
I WAS SO IN SHOCK THAT I HAD A RANDOM FLASHBACK!

EXCUSE ME ...
I'll try talking to him.

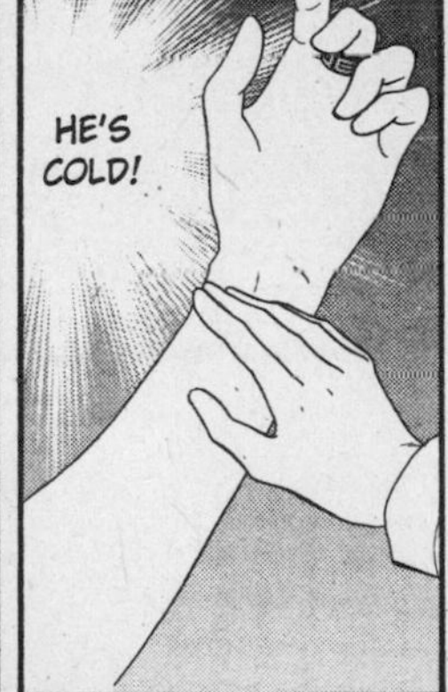
HE'S COLD!

THERE'S NO PULSE! HE'S NOT BREATHING!! THEN HE *IS* A DOLL!
BUT HE LOOKS SO HUMAN... NO, WAIT!
I-IS HE DEAD!?

WHAT SHOULD I DO!?
I HAVE TO TALK TO SOMEONE ...
SOSHI ...

!?
BEEP
HELLO! GAKU NAMIKIRI HERE! ♪
HEY, YOU!
THANKS FOR ORDERING FROM THE LOVER SHOP! SO, YOU LIKE? ♪
DID YOU SEND ME A CADAVER!?
Is this some kind of murder mystery!?
HUH? WHAT ARE YOU TALKING ABOUT?
YOU GOTTA READ THE MANUAL, DARLIN'!
A *DEAD* BODY WOULDN'T BE SO SOFT.
I'LL CALL YOU AGAIN IN THREE DAYS.
WHAT !?
W-WAIT!

MANUAL
?
FWAP
WHAT'S THIS? "NO DANGER OF PREGNANCY"? THAT'S DISGUSTING!!
HERE WE GO! "GETTING STARTED" ...
IT MOVES
?
FOR REAL !?
THAT'S WHAT IT SAYS ...

FIRST, ACTIVATE THE UNIT.

BA-BUMP

BA-BUMP

Rolled him over.

I-I HAVE TO TOUCH IT?

BA-BUMP

BA-BUMP

BA-BUMP

THAT WEIRD GUY WAS RIGHT--HE DOES FEEL SOFT.

HE EVEN HAS MOLES.

PAT PAT

IS THIS A DOLL OR A PERSON ?

BA-BUMP

I'VE NEVER EVEN KISSED A REAL BOY BEFORE...
BA-BUMP
THE UNIT'S LIPS ARE EQUIPPED WITH A SENSOR...
BA-BUM
BA-BUMP
...THAT DETECTS THE BODY HEAT FROM YOUR LIPS...
SHOULD I... DO IT?
WHAT'VE I GOT TO LOSE?
BA-BUMP
BA-BUMP
...
BA-BUMP

...AND REGISTERS YOU AS HIS LOVER.
DO IT!!

WHIRR

BA-BUMP

FWASH

BA-BUM

TWITCH

BA-BUMP

BA-BUMP
BA-BUMP
HE MOVED !!
BA-BUMP
OH... MY... GOD...

SMILE
IT'S A PLEASURE TO MEET YOU...
...GIRL-FRIEND.
WHAT THE...?
AM I DREAMING!?

Act 2 Three-day Boyfriend

2003.04
OH MY GOSH ...
A MAN-NEQUIN JUST SAT UP AND KISSED ME!!
FROZEN
"GO TO THIS WEB-SITE."
恋 Lover
SHOP
"WE HAVE THE IDEAL LOVER WHO EXISTS JUST FOR YOU."

I DON'T KNOW WHAT I EXPECTED WHEN I PLACED MY ORDER, BUT THIS IS...
WOULD YOU LIKE TO KEEP GOING?
GULP
HALT!!
HMM?
WHAT *ARE* YOU !?
A ROBOT? ONE OF THOSE DUDES FROM A.I. !?
UMF

WHAT ELSE?
I'M YOUR BOYFRIEND.
GASP
Eek!
COVER YOURSELF!!
LIKE THIS?
NOT YOUR FACE!!
JUST TURN AROUND! I'LL FIND YOU SOME CLOTHES!!
WHAM
UM, UM...
DAD MUST HAVE SOMETHING...

DING-DONG

DING-DONG

THIS IS WHEN SOSHI COMES BY!!

UH-OH...

CHAK

WAP

WUMP
STAY IN THERE !!

SHHH!!
SHHH?

KLAK

WHAT ?
HUFF
HUFF

NOTHING ...I JUST...
I BROUGHT YOU SOME TAKE-OUT.
THANKS !!

Well...
I'D BETTER CLEAN YOUR ROOM AGAIN.
WAP
W-WAIT!!

YOU CLEANED IT YESTER-DAY! IT'S FINE!
HMPH. SURE, IF YOU'RE A PIG.
I'LL DO IT MY-SELF!!

I'VE TURNED OVER A NEW LEAF!!
RIIKO, WHAT ARE YOU SO NERVOUS ABOUT?

Ah...
ATCHOO

HEY!! IS SOME-ONE IN THERE!?
NO, THERE ISN'T!!
BUT I JUST HEARD...

YOU'RE HEARING THINGS!! YOU'RE TOO TIRED!!
NOT *THAT* TIRED!
OKAY, GOOD-NIGHT!
BUT IT'S EARLY!
WHUP WHUP WHUP
IS SHE STILL UPSET OVER ISHIZEKI?
WHAM
UM, HEY!
DOOM
OH, SORRY ABOUT THAT!
WHY DOES A DOLL HAVE TO SNEEZE?
UH, I DON'T KNOW...

ANYWAY, YOU HAVE THREE FULL DAYS TO ENJOY ME!

I'M ALL YOURS.

THAT'S RIGHT.

SPECIAL PROMOTIO
7-DAY FREE TRIAL OFFER
TRY IT AND SEE
YOURSELF!

HE'LL BE HERE FOR THREE DAYS...

WHAT WOULD YOU LIKE ME TO DO NOW?

UM, NOTHING. I'M SUDDENLY VERY TIRED.

I THINK I'LL GO TO BED...

OH

HEY, GIRL-FRIEND.
COME HERE.
SWUP
!!
WH-WHAT ARE YOU DOING !?
You're naked again !!
WELL, YOU SAID YOU WANTED TO GO TO BED.
I'm ready.
WHAT !?

WELL, YOU KNOW ...

I *AM* FROM THE NIGHTLY LOVER SERIES.

HOLD ON!
SNAP
THINGS ARE MOVING TOO FAST ...
SNAP
N--
NO!!
KRAK
I DON'T TAKE LOVE SO LIGHTLY, BUDDY!!
SURE, I'M CURIOUS ABOUT SEX...

...BUT I WANT TO EXPERIENCE ROMANCE FIRST!
SEX SHOULD COME **AFTER** WE'RE IN LOVE!!
SO, I CAN'T DO THIS... YET!!
HUFF HUFF HUFF HUFF
ALL RIGHT.
I UNDERSTAND.
!
A BOYFRIEND...
...NEVER FORCES HIMSELF ON HIS GIRL.

SO, GIRL-FRIEND ...
WHAT'S YOUR NAME?

Ohh...
RIIKO ...
... IZAWA.
THAT'S A PRETTY NAME. WILL YOU GIVE ME A GOOD NAME, TOO?

WHAT ?
WHAT'S MY NAME ?
A BOY-FRIEND SHOULD HAVE A NAME.

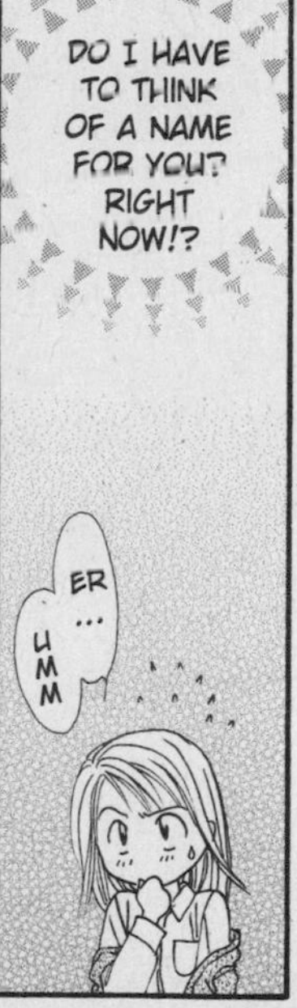
DO I HAVE TO THINK OF A NAME FOR YOU? RIGHT NOW!?
ER ... UMM

AHA!
nighty
THE BOX HE WAS IN SAID...

..."NIGHT"!
NO IMAGINA-TION.
HOW DOES "NIGHT" SOUND !?

NIGHT...
AHH...
I LOVE IT!
THE NEXT THREE DAYS ARE GONNA BE GREAT, RIIKO!
EEK!!
IT'D KEEP MY MIND OFF THINGS IF I HAD SOMEONE WITH ME...
BUT YOU'LL HAVE TO SLEEP IN MY PARENTS' ROOM...
OKAY!
SO MANY SUR-PRISES... BUT HE SEEMS NICE.
"SORRY."
"I LIKE SOME-ONE ELSE!!"
THROB
OH, NO!!

I agree that guys with glasses can look hot. And before this, I'd only put bad guys (Kagami from *Ceres*) and side characters in glasses, so I felt pretty good about Soshi. (By the way, my editor tells me there are a lot of Soshi fans on the editorial staff.) Soshi doesn't smile very much. I like guys like him (smile).

Night, of course, is the character I first thought of and the crux of this story. Basically the only thing that changed about him from my initial vision is the side his hair is parted on (smile). I was inspired by a Beauness Skin Care commercial that starred Naohito Fujiki. Which means he's the soothing type. (Was it my subconscious desire to be soothed!?) He seems more and more like an airhead as time goes on. Now he's like a pet dog--kind of cute and innocent and very devoted. My assistant just said, "I'd buy one if they actually existed. Definitely." (For $1 million.)

Heck, I'd buy one, too! (smile). Maybe I'd put him to work as one of my assistants (smile). I called him a "figure" because "robot" would've been too stiff and wasn't quite the image I had for Night. Also, we don't really know if he's robotic or not. What is he made out of? A "figure" is a likeness of a person. He may be a doll, but he's as close to human as you can get, so I think it's the term that fits the best.

The real world of collectible anime action figures is pretty intense. It seems interesting, though. My assistant J is making a Night figurine (so I hear). But will she ever get it done? If she does, I'd like to include a picture to show everyone. A miniature Night. He'd have to be naked, of course. It's lots of fun to draw naked guys. Whoa there.

HEY! RIIKO, TODAY AFTER SCHOOL ...
OH, SORRY, MIKA. I CAN'T TODAY!
I COULDN'T SLEEP. I KEPT THINKING, "THERE'S A GUY IN THE NEXT ROOM!"
I'LL BUY HIM SOME CLOTHES ON THE WAY HOME.
DAD'S PAJAMAS AREN'T QUITE THE RIGHT LOOK FOR HIM.
RUSTLE
COMES WITH CLOTHES.
...
Bictoria
I HOPE THESE PANTS FIT.

ISHIZEKI !?
GASP
WIP
I HEARD YOU REALLY BLEW OFF THAT GIRL!
URK
YEAH, YOU SHOULD'VE SEEN HER FACE.
HEY. TELL ME ALL ABOUT IT IN THE CAFÉ.
BA-BUMP
BA-BUMP
KRK
BA-BU

BA-BUMP

!

RIIKO!?

TMP

BA-BUMP

BA-BUMP

WHAT WOULD YOU LIKE?

Um...

I'LL HAVE THIS, AND THIS!

Uh...

I'LL HAVE ICED TEA.

COMING RIGHT UP.
BA-BUMP

BA-BUMP
SO, SHE AMBUSHED YOU, HUH?
...
Yeah.
SHE CAUGHT ME AT THE BUS STOP.

BA-BUMP
BUT I SAW IT COMING, SO I WAS READY TO DITCH HER OFF THE BAT.

ISHI-ZEKI !?
MOMMY, LOOK!
WHAT IS IT?

ACK!
TUMP
THUD

SHOOM
HE JUST...
MY HERO!
MOMMY?
A two-year fan of kids' action shows
RIIKO IZAWA?
SHE'S NOT MY TYPE. SHE'S *NOTHING* LIKE MY GIRL.
What?
YOU'VE GOT A GIRL!?

AND YOU WOULDN'T BELIEVE WHAT ELSE ...
WHAT!? SHE WAS CARRYING HER BRA? WHAT A FREAK!
HA HA HA HA
WAS IT A PRESENT FOR YOU?
HEH, I DON'T KNOW. SHE'S SO WEIRD ...
SPLASH
PFFT!!
GRR
RIIKO !?

WH- WHAT ARE YOU DOING HERE?
WHAT THE HECK ?
You got us wet!!
KLINK
...
YOU'RE A TOTAL JERK!
WHAT DID I EVER SEE IN YOU?
WHAT'S YOUR PROBLEM ?
WERE YOU STALKING ME? WHAT A LOSER!
WHAT DID I EVER SEE IN YOU?
SHE'S PSYCHO!
NO WONDER YOU CAN'T GET A DATE!
MY VOICE ...
THE WORDS WON'T COME OUT!

DARN IT!
I CAN'T LET THEM SEE ME CRY.
STOP IT!!
DON'T CRY!!
WUP
HEY ...
FWASH
WHAT'S WRONG ?

DID THAT BOY...
...MAKE YOU CRY?

SHWAK
ISHI-ZEKI!!
IF YOU MAKE MY GIRL-FRIEND CRY AGAIN...
...YOU'LL GET WORSE THAN THAT!

LET'S GO, RIIKO.
WHO WAS THAT GUY!?
ARE YOU OKAY?
DON'T JUST STAND THERE, HELP HIM!
...
ARE YOU ALL RIGHT?
SIR?
GRIN
?

WHAM
ARGH!
ASAMOTO! WHY ARE YOU HIT-TING THE CUSTOMERS !?
SORRY, I QUIT.
WHO ... WAS THAT GUY ?

NIGHT, HOW DID YOU KNOW WHERE I WAS!?
'CAUSE I'M YOUR BOY-FRIEND. PLEASE DON'T CRY.
...
FOR THREE DAYS ...
...HE'LL BE MY BOY-FRIEND.
LOOKS LIKE HE'S DOING FINE!
HEH

Absolute
Boyfriend

Act 3
The Purchase

WHAM
WE'RE HOME!
NO-BODY'S HERE BUT US!
NOW WHAT, RIIKO? ARE YOU HUNGRY?
NO, I THINK I'LL GO TO BED... ER, RETIRE.
THANKS FOR WHAT YOU DID.
SWIP
GOOD-NIGHT!

THUD
SHE'S STILL SAD ...
"I SAW IT COMING SO I WAS READY TO DITCH HER OFF THE BAT."
"SHE'S NOT MY TYPE."
"SHE'S SO WEIRD."
P25US
DoCoNo

"WHAT A LOSER!"
"NO WONDER YOU CAN'T GET A DATE!"
THEY'RE RIGHT.
I'M AWK-WARD, MEDIOCRE AND WORTH-LESS.
NO GUY WOULD EVER GO OUT WITH ME...
WHUP
TMP
I WONDER IF RIIKO'S HOME.

I'VE GOTTA FIND OUT ...
...WHO THAT GUY IS.
TWEET

SWIP
BONK
UGH!
CHAK
OOPS.
I SLEPT WITH MY CLOTHES ON...
Oh.
GOOD MORNING, RIIKO.

You see, for some reason I declared to everyone that, starting in 2003, I'd be specializing in drawing men! And now I actually find that I'm not in the mood to draw female characters. That's not good!! I've always been asked why I portray the female body like I do given, that I'm a female artist. A lot of people have told me that the girls I draw look soft--especially their breasts. What happened to me!? I look back fondly on the days when I put so much effort into curves. My male readers appreciated it, too. But something changed in me, I guess. (I don't really understand it (smile). I still like sexy women, though... Hmm, maybe it's about "sexiness." Riiko's not very sexy (smile). It's not that I stopped caring. I'm just focusing more on the male characters.

Anyway, I think "unsexy" Riiko is actually pretty cute. She's so natural and says exactly what's on her mind. As I was working on the first episode, I felt like I wanted her as a friend (smile). She's such a slob! And she'd be like that in real life. Or even worse (smile)!!

By the way, the comedy routines are exactly like ours at home (smile). My workplace is full of comedy! I can be silly sometimes, but I prefer to be the straight man.

I got letters from astute readers who noticed that all the names (in the Japanese) are written in *katakana*.* Yes, that was intentional. I did that so they'd all match Night's name, and also to create kind of a futuristic feel (since Night is a futuristic character). I always try to put something different in my newest work. It's a pretty minor thing, though.

*The Japanese use *katakana* symbols to write foreign words.

HERE.
SAY "AAH!" ♡
BA-BUMP
HUH!? THAT'S OKAY !!
AAH.
...
CHOMP

IT'S DELI- CIOUS!
WOW! YOU'RE EVEN A GOOD COOK!
? ISN'T THAT WHAT YOU ORDERED ?
OH
PERSONALITY OPTIONS
PLEASE SELECT THE QUALITIES OF YOUR IDEAL LOVER.
OH YEAH, I DID ADD A BUNCH OF STUFF.
WHAT ELSE DID I SELECT ?
THERE'S NO SCHOOL TODAY, RIGHT ?
LET'S GO OUT TOGE- THER. IT'S A BEAUTI- FUL DAY!
I'M NOT SURE I'M IN THE MOOD ...
NO? WELL, THEN ...
WE CAN JUST STAY HERE AND HAVE SEX.
LET'S GO OUT! PLEASE !!

WOW.
I FEEL KIND OF COOL.
ALL THE GIRLS ARE CHECKING HIM OUT...

YOU RARELY SEE SUCH COOL-LOOKING GUYS.
...EVEN THOUGH HE ISN'T HUMAN.
LOOK.

STRAWHAT
THIS WOULD LOOK GREAT ON YOU.
Y-YOU THINK SO?
DEFINITELY!
WITH YOUR SKIN, ANY COLOR WOULD LOOK GOOD.

THIS ONE?
KLAK
I'LL GIVE IT A TRY.

HE'S TOO GOOD.

HE'S WINNING TOO MUCH.

FEELING BETTER NOW?

YES.

ONE-HUNDRED PERCENT ACCURACY... TOP SCORE?

OH, WAIT, I GOT A MESSAGE...

NOT SO FAST, KIDDO!

WHUMP

!!
SHOOM
MY PICTURE OF ISHI-ZEKI...
P25US
DoCoNo
!!
KLAK

HE FLEW !!
WHOA!
OH! MY HERO!
TOMP

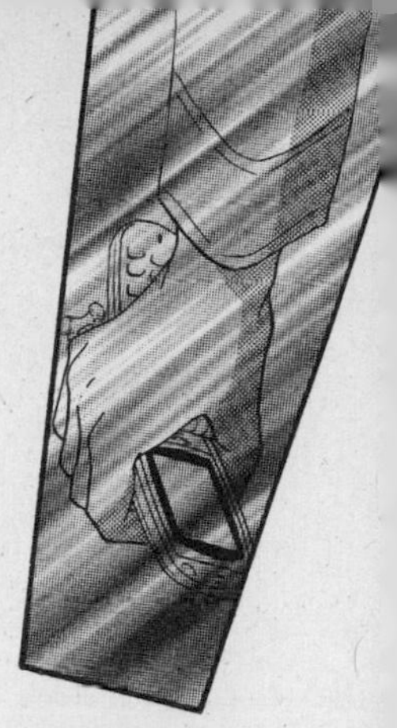

TUMP

OOH!
KLAP KLAP
KLAP
IS HE A STUNT-MAN !?
MY HERO !!
WOW!
KLAP KLAP
KLAP
NIGHT !!

RIIKO!
ARE YOU OKAY!? YOU WERE SO HIGH...
THAT'S DANGER-OUS.
Even if you're not human!!

THIS MEANS A LOT TO YOU, DOESN'T IT?
I'M FINE!
YOU'RE SO COOL!
Oh.
THANKS!
HEH
HA HA HA
YOU ACT LIKE IT WAS NOTHING!
YOU'RE INCREDIBLE, NIGHT!
THANKS !!

FWASH
WHAT?
YOU ARE FEELING BETTER.
YOU FINALLY SMILED.
THAT MAKES ME HAPPY.

YOU'RE EVEN PRETTIER WHEN YOU SMILE.
BLUSH
DON'T LIE!
HUH? BUT "LIAR" WASN'T ONE OF THE OPTIONS YOU SELECTED.
...
Okay.
NEXT, WE'LL GO...
IT'S SO WEIRD.
MY HEART IS RACING...
HEY! U LOOKED SO
NOT LIKE U!
o(><)o
LET'S PARTY SOON!
MIKA ...

KLIK
KLIK
P25US
CHEER UP, K?
:P
SOSHI
...
SH25US
FROM: RIIKO
TO: SOSHI
DON'T WORRY,
I'M TOUGH!
THANKS
...
HEH

P35US
DoCoNo
DELET

BEEP

KNOCK KNOCK

RIIKO ?

UM...
COULD I...
...STAY WITH YOU TO-NIGHT?
AH!
BUT NOT TO HAVE SEX!
...
JUST ...
...YOU KNOW ...
WUP

COME HERE.

YOU'RE SO WARM.
THANK YOU ...
... NIGHT.
BLINK

GASP
GOOD MORNING.
IT'S MORNING!
WERE YOU AWAKE ALL NIGHT!? DON'T YOU SLEEP!?
ACK!
I CAN SLEEP, BUT...
I WAS WATCHING YOU.
AFTER ALL, THIS IS OUR LAST DAY TOGETHER.
OH!
THAT'S RIGHT.
I'D FORGOTTEN.

NIGHT ONLY HAD THREE DAYS.

PROMOTIONAL OFFER THREE-DAY FREE TRIAL

TOMOR-ROW I HAVE TO RETURN HIM.

ARE YOU SURE YOU DON'T WANT TO HAVE SEX?

...

I FEEL ...

...A LITTLE ...

...SAD.

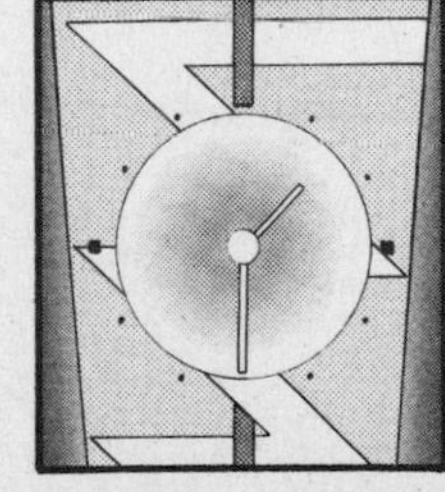

...JUST A LITTLE LONGER ...

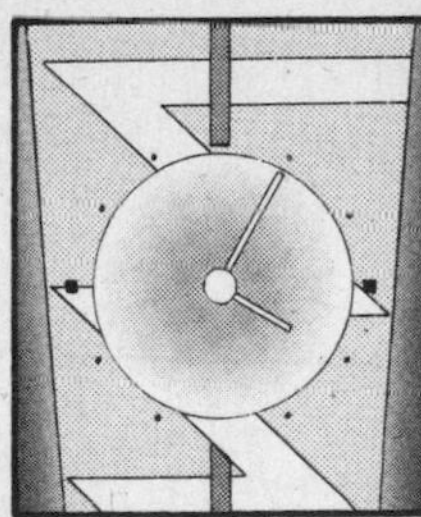

DING-DONG DING-DONG

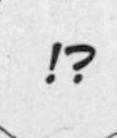

HI THERE !!
KRONOS HEAVEN APPRECIATES YOUR BUSINESS!
YOU !!
THAT COS-PLAYING SALES-MAN !!
I'M NOT COSPLAYING!
ANYHOW, MISS ...

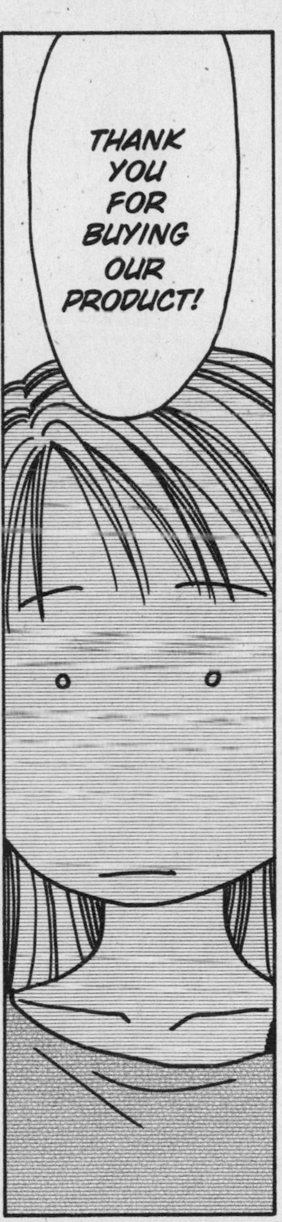
THANK YOU FOR BUYING OUR PRODUCT!

HUH?
RIIKO?
I'M TALKING ABOUT HIM, OF COURSE!
THE FIGURE YOU BOUGHT FROM OUR LOVER SHOP!

WHAT!? *BOUGHT*?
BUT IT WAS A THREE-DAY FREE TRIAL...
DON'T WORRY, OUR COMPANY WOULD NEVER RIP YOU OFF!

WAIT ...
WE'VE DECIDED TO GIVE YOU A SPECIAL BARGAIN-BASEMENT DISCOUNT!!
BUT ...

FOR YOU, ONLY ONE MILLION DOLLARS!!

A MILLION DOLLARS!?
WHAT IS?
YOU ARE.
AW, COME ON. DIDN'T YOU READ THE CON-TRACT?
THE FREE TRIAL WAS FOR THREE DAYS-- EXACTLY 72 HOURS FROM TIME OF DELIVERY-- WHICH ENDED AT 4:05 P.M. TODAY!
RIIKO
YOU DIDN'T RETURN IT BY THAT TIME, SO...
...YOU BOUGHT IT!
YOU OWE US ONE MILLION DOLLARS!!
WHAT THE ...?

Absolute
Boyfriend

Act 4
The Million-Dollar Man

HE COSTS A MILLION DOLLARS!?
$1 MILLION
THAT'S RIGHT!!
YOU DIDN'T RETURN HIM WITHIN 72 HOURS, SO YOU AGREED TO BUY HIM.
B-BUT WHY IS HE SO EXPENSIVE, MR. GUNKY MANTID-ITTY!?
THAT'S GAKU NAMI-KIRI!
SO...
▲Stuff that Night prepared.

LOOK, SON. HERE'S A $100 BILL!!
Fwip
YOU'RE WORTH TEN THOUSAND OF THESE!
WOW, THAT'S A LOT, PROBABLY!!
YEP, YOU'RE A MILLION-DOLLAR MAN!

AND *SHE'S* GOTTA PAY UP!
THANKS, RIIKO!
Wow!
BUT I DON'T HAVE A MILLION DOLLARS!!

Huh?
WHAT'RE YOU TALKING ABOUT?

CHECK OUT THIS HERE LIST OF PERSONALITY OPTIONS!!
TAH-DAH
Riiko Izawa
OPTIONS!?
HA!
OH YEAH, I ADDED A FEW THINGS...

EACH OPTION COSTS $10,000 ...
• A LITTLE POSSESSIVE
• TAKES CHARGE
• COMFORTING
• CHARMING
• SUPER NICE AND KIND!!
• DEPENDABLE
• GREAT COOK
• ATHLETIC
• GOOFY (IN A CUTE WAY)
• MANLY (MAKES ME DO THE RIGHT THING)
• A LITTLE HORNY
• ALWAYS WINS A FISTFIGHT!
• CLEAN
• ALWAYS COMES TO MY RESCUE!!
• HANDY
• SMART
• CUTE
• STYLISH
A MILLION BUCKS IS CHEAP FOR ALL THIS!
ACK
OH, THAT!

I'M SUCH AN IDIOT ...
KIND OF GREEDY, HUH !?
A GUY LIKE THAT WOULD BE A FREAK IF HE REALLY EXISTED!
I guess he does exist now.
AWRIGHT, IF YOU DON'T HAVE THE CASH, YOU CAN PAY IN INSTALL-MENTS!
HERE'S A CONVENIENT 50-YEAR PAYMENT PLAN...
munch munch
FIFTY YEARS!?

MY LIFE IS OVER.
SORRY, IT'S TOO LATE TO RETURN HIM.
ALL RIGHT, THEN I'LL PAY!
SNAP
HOW'RE YOU GONNA PAY FOR YOURSELF, DUMMY !?

HMM, WE DEVELOPED HIM IN THE FIRST PLACE TO SELL TO WEALTHY HOUSE-WIVES.
I DON'T SEE HOW YOU COULD PART WITH HIM AFTER TRYING HIM OUT FOR THREE DAYS.
HUH?
HE KNOWS TECHNIQUES THAT COULD SEND YOU TO PARADISE!
Aw, don't make me say any more. It's embarrassing!
BUT WE HAVEN'T DONE ANYTHING.
Not a thing...
Y'ALL DIDN'T DO THE FLABBY!? DUMMY!! THAT'S WHAT HE'S FOR!!
HE'S FROM THE NIGHTLY LOVER SERIES!! HE CAN DO IT 30 TIMES IN ONE NIGHT!!
You'd die.
STOP! I'M INTO ROMANTIC LOVE FIRST AND FOREMOST, OKAY!?
HUH? I JUST CAN'T UNDERSTAND WOMEN. WHAT DO I DO, DR. PHIL?
YOU'RE CALLING FOR ADVICE !?
IF ONLY THERE WAS SOME-ONE I COULD CALL!!

ANY-WAY, YOU'VE GOTTA PAY!

HERE ARE THE TERMS OF THE 50-YEAR PLAN.

W-WAIT ...

NOW, DON'T YOU TRY TO WEASEL OUT OF IT!

THE FIRST PAYMENT OF $300 IS DUE IN THREE DAYS!

WHAT AM I GONNA DO!?

...

I CAN'T PAY A MILLION DOLLARS !!

SHOULD I CALL MY PARENTS?
Uh...
MOM, DAD, I DID SOME INTERNET SHOPPING...
...AND I DON'T HAVE ENOUGH TO COVER THE BILL... HOW MUCH, YOU ASK?
A MILLION DOLLARS!!
※Father was transferred abroad. Mother works for the media.
DARN.
THEY'LL DISOWN ME...
And they'll both have heart attacks.
I'LL HAVE TO GO TO WORK...
THERE'S ONLY ONE WAY FOR A TEENAGE GIRL TO EARN THAT MUCH MONEY IN THREE DAYS...
CONSTRUCTION WORK.
MOST PEOPLE WOULD'VE GUESSED SOMETHING ELSE!!
SNAP
Yuck.
I THOUGHT YOU LEFT!
YOU NEEDED SOME COMIC RELIEF.
Get lost!
...RIIKO.

WHAT ?
MAYBE I SHOULD DO SOME-THING.
LIKE WHAT ?
I COULD GET A JOB! I COULD PAY FOR MYSELF!
THAT SOUNDS WEIRD.
BUT ...
I CAN'T SIT HERE AND DO NOTHING.
NIGHT ...
IT'S MY FAULT FOR NOT READING THE CONTRACT CAREFULLY.
...I'LL FIGURE SOMETHING OUT. DON'T WORRY!
RIIKO ...

Next up: Gaku Namikiri. Here's another character who speaks in the Kansai dialect. My very first series didn't allow for this, of course, but I wanted to include a character that speaks the dialect in every one of my series. I'm from Osaka, but I've lived in Tokyo for a long time. Someday, I'll have lived in Tokyo longer than the 20 years I lived in Osaka. I don't use my Kansai dialect with anyone besides my family now, but I do use it in my manga how-to column, "It's Academic!" which is running in *Shojo Comics*, to make myself stand out. These days, I even talk to myself in standard Japanese half the time. When I go home to Osaka, I obviously talk to my friends in the Kansai dialect, but now it takes me three days to get used to it. Sometimes I think I shouldn't be so affected by everything Tokyo! Nah, I'm not affected. See, the fact that I play the straight man is proof that I'm pure Kansai! I have to have my Kansai characters to stay connected to my roots!

So who is Gaku, anyway? (smile). My assistants think he should be in his late twenties. Kronos Heaven is mysterious, too. Actually, I haven't given it much thought. ← Hey!!! Well, I'll just say it's a secret for now (smile).

Absolute Boyfriend isn't supposed to be very complicated. I'm just writing everything in the spirit of the moment, whether it's fun, excitement, serious drama or whatever. So, I hope my readers won't take it too seriously and will just enjoy what happens. Anyway, it's a romantic comedy at heart, of course. But will Riiko end up with Night or Soshi? No, seriously, I don't know myself!

MONEY?
YOU'RE LOOKING FOR A JOB?
YEAH. KNOW ANYTHING THAT PAYS WELL?
PROSTITUTION!
Just kidding!
HA HA HA
HEE HEE HEE
IS THAT MY ONLY CHOICE?
NOBODY WOULD PAY YOU FOR THAT.
Flatsy.
DOES SOMEONE NEED ANOTHER LESSON IN MANNERS!?
SOSHI!! HOW LONG HAVE YOU BEEN STANDING THERE!?
I WAS JUST PASSING BY. I HAVE STUFF TO DO.

WHAT STUFF?
DON'T PUT ANY WILD IDEAS IN RIIKO'S HEAD.
SHE'S LIABLE TO TAKE THEM SERIOUSLY.

Geez...
ARE YOU IN LOVE WITH HER OR SOMETHING?

TWITCH

HUH?

DON'T EVEN SAY THAT, MIKA!

YOU'RE GONNA FINISH HIM SOMEDAY, RIIKO.

TOMP TOMP

UGH

ERK

SO...

WHY DO YOU NEED MONEY?

THOOM

EEP!

UM, WELL... YOU KNOW...

I-I BOUGHT SOME-THING ONLINE...
WHAT WAS IT?
HOW MUCH WAS IT?
A LIFE-SIZE ANIMATED SEX DOLL... FOR A MILLION BUCKS.
MENTAL IMAGE
THAT DOESN'T SOUND SO GOOD, DOES IT...?
I-IT'S A SECRET!
YOU HAVE A JOB, RIGHT, SOSHI?
YOU SAID IT PAYS WELL.
WELL, THEY MAY HAVE AN OPEN-ING...
...SINCE I QUIT.
WHAT?

OH YEAH, THERE'S BEEN NO FOOD ...

I BROUGHT YOU SOME-THING.

...FOR THE LAST COUPLE OF DAYS.

WHY'D YOU QUIT ?

...

GLANCE
?
NO REASON.
DING-DONG
C'MON, IT'S TIME FOR CLASS.
?
...

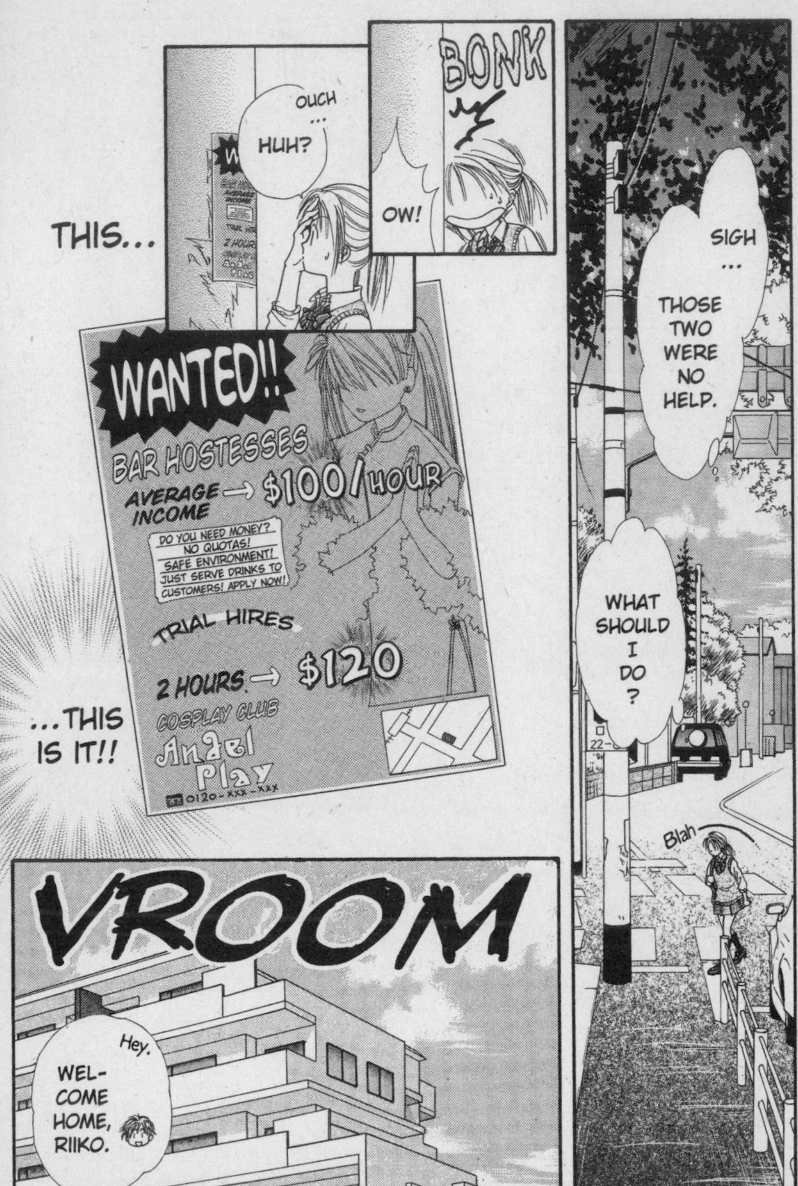
SIGH ...
THOSE TWO WERE NO HELP.
WHAT SHOULD I DO ?
Blah
BONK
OW!
OUCH ...
HUH?
THIS...
WANTED!!
BAR HOSTESSES
AVERAGE INCOME → $100/HOUR
DO YOU NEED MONEY? NO QUOTAS! SAFE ENVIRONMENT! JUST SERVE DRINKS TO CUSTOMERS! APPLY NOW!
TRIAL HIRES
2 HOURS → $120
COSPLAY CLUB
Angel Play
0120-XXX-XXX
...THIS IS IT!!
VROOM
Hey.
WEL-COME HOME, RIIKO.

WHAM
WANT TO SHOWER FIRST OR HAVE DINNER ?
SHOOM
NIGHT, GUARD THE APARTMENT, OKAY!?
Or have sex?
...
MY NAME IS RIIKO TZAWA, I'M 18 YEARS OLD,
AND I'M A VERY HARD WORKER !!
Padded Bra
ARE YOU SURE YOU'RE OUT OF HIGH SCHOOL?
STARE
Well...
I'M SHORT OF PEOPLE TONIGHT, SO I'LL GIVE YOU A CHANCE!
GREAT!

THANK YOU VERY MUCH!

YES!!

NIGHT !?
WHAT ARE YOU DOING HERE !?
Uh?
DO YOU WANT A JOB, TOO?
Author's license

NIGHT, YOU CAN'T! BESIDES, ONLY GIRLS WORK HERE...
Really?

YOU'RE VERY PRETTY!
PUT ON A DRESS AND YOU'VE GOT A JOB!!
WHAT? ...

BUT...
WHAT THE HELL ...
...IS THIS OUT-FIT !?
Does this reek of manga geek or what!?
HOW DO I LOOK ?
MAID OUTFIT
RIIKO! RIIKO!
YOU LOOK TOO GOOD !!
Deflated.
Riiko?
Oh my!
OH WELL, I'LL HAVE TO BITE THE BULLET!!
I'VE GOTTA PAY THAT BILL!!

ON SECOND THOUGHT, I WANNA GO HOME!!

LOOK AT THESE WEIRDOS ...

WELL, ALL I HAVE TO DO IS SERVE DRINKS.
NICE TO MEET YOU.
Wow!
HOW DO YOU DO? YOU'RE HOT!

HMPH... OF COURSE HE'S PERFECT--HE'S ARTIFICIAL.
GLUG GLUG GLUG
Hey watch it!

Oops.
I'M SORRY!
Hey...
THAT'S OKAY, KITTEN!
YOU'RE CLUMSY, BUT CUTE!!
ERK
EEK!
WHAK
KRASH
WHAT ARE YOU DOING TO THE CUSTOM-ERS!?
Mumble...
HE HAD IT COMING.
RIIKO'S MY GIRL-FRIEND.
NIGHT...
AW...

I-IT'S NO BIG DEAL...
I NEED THIS JOB, NIGHT!
ALL RIGHT, FOLKS. THE WAIT IS OVER!!
GULP
IT'S SHOW-TIME!!

OH MY GOSH!

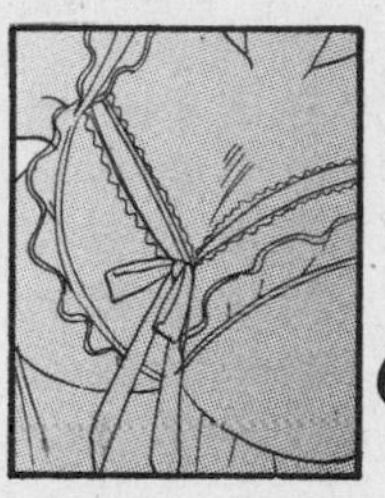

THIS IS...

...A STRIP CLUB!

FW
UP
!!
HEY!!
STOP THAT!!
WHAK

THAT'S MY GIRL!
DON'T YOU TOUCH HER !!
HE'S ... ...A GUY.
NIGHT ...
YOU'RE SAFE NOW, RIIKO!
WHOMP
LET ME TAKE CARE OF THAT GUY!!
NIGHT, STOP!!
HUH? I KNOW HOW TO DO THIS. I HAVE A GENTLE TOUCH.
THAT'S NOT THE PROB-LEM !!

ARGH!
WHAT ARE YOU DOING!?
This isn't that kind of bar!
YOU'RE BOTH FIRED!!

DIDN'T MAKE ONE CENT.
I'M SORRY, RIIKO...
You don't even know why you got yelled at...
IT'S OKAY. I DIDN'T REALIZE IT WAS THAT KIND OF PLACE.

BUT WE DIDN'T MAKE ANY MONEY...
NO, WE DIDN'T...
HA HA
I GUESS I'LL HAVE TO ROB A BANK OR SOME-THING!

AM I GOING TO HAVE TO SELL MY BODY?
RIIKO...

I WANT YOU ...
...TO RETURN ME.
WHAT?
GAKU NAMIKIRI MAY PUT UP A FIGHT...
...BUT I'LL TALK TO HIM.

BUT ...
SURE, IT WOULD GET ME OUT OF THIS MESS, BUT...
I DON'T WANT ...
...YOU TO SACRIFICE YOURSELF FOR ME.
I WANT YOU TO BE HAPPY.
SO... PLEASE RETURN ME!

BA-BUMP
BA-BUMP
STOP BLUSHING. THIS IS JUST ANOTHER OPTION YOU SELECTED.
BA-BUMP
BUT...
UH...
...THEN WHAT WILL HAPPEN TO YOU?
...
IT DOESN'T MATTER.
I WANT TO DO IT FOR YOU.
DON'T LOOK SO SAD.
AND DON'T SAY THINGS LIKE THAT.

BA-BUMP
BA-BUMP
BA-BUMP
I...
I...
HE REALLY IS A WELL-MADE PRODUCT...
WHAP
...IF I DO SAY SO MYSELF!
JUST LISTEN TO HIM TALK!
GAKU !?
Where did you come from !?
HOW'S BUSINESS? OH, BUT I GUESS THAT DOESN'T APPLY TO YOU!

AW, WELL, WHAT'RE YOU GONNA DO?
I COULD GIVE YOU A SPECIAL BARGAIN PRICE!
WHAT?
JUST GIVE ME ALL THE MONEY YOU'VE GOT!
R-REALLY!?
ON ONE CONDITION.
YOU'VE GOTTA...
...OFFER YOURSELF TO OUR COMPANY!
WHAT!?

Act 5 Dinner

WELL?

WHAT DO YOU MEAN...
...I HAVE TO SELL MYSELF TO YOU!?

HUH?
WHO SAID ANYTHING ABOUT THAT?
YOU DID! BACK THERE!
YOU SAID YOU'D GIVE ME A DISCOUNT ON NIGHT...

...IF I OFFERED MYSELF TO YOUR COMPANY!
OH, THAT? THAT'S NOT WHAT I MEANT!

ANYHOW, YOU DON'T HAVE MUCH THERE TO SELL!
GRRR
EASY, RIIKO!
WHAT WE WANT IS DATA.
DATA?
HE'S A QUALITY PRODUCT, RIGHT?
BUT HE'S JUST A PROTOTYPE. THERE ARE SOME DETAILS WE STILL HAVE TO IRON OUT.
THE IDEA WAS TO PLEASE WOMEN.
WE CAN GIVE HIM ALL THE RIGHT PHYSICAL FEATURES ...
...BUT WE NEED A BETTER UNDER-STANDING OF THE FEMALE MIND.
YOU DON'T WANT TO HAVE SEX WITHOUT LOVE, RIGHT?

WOMEN SURE ARE COMPLI-CATED!
WE CAN'T CREATE THE PERFECT MALE UNTIL WE FIGURE YOU WOMEN OUT!
THAT'S WHERE YOU COME IN!!

WE'LL WRITE OFF YOUR DEBT IF YOU TEACH HIM EVERY-THING THERE IS TO KNOW ABOUT WOMEN!!

EVERY-THING !?
EVERY SINGLE THING!?
THE PSYCHO-LOGICAL AND THE PHYSICAL.
WE'LL USE THE DATA IN OUR FUTURE MODELS.

THAT'S LIKE ASKING ME TO GET NAKED WITH HIM.
No way!

HAVE YOU GOT A MILLION DOLLARS ?
NO.

GATHERING DATA IS EASY. NIGHT, GIVE ME YOUR LEFT HAND.

SEE THIS RING?
IT READS HUMAN EMOTIONS. THE STONE IN THE MIDDLE IS USUALLY WHITE.

IT TURNS RED FOR HAPPINESS, BLUE FOR ANGER, AND BLACK FOR SADNESS.
Oh, and...
PINK IS FOR PLEA-SURE!
HMPH!

GIVE HIM AS MUCH DATA AS YOU CAN UNTIL WE COMPLETE OUR NEXT MODEL...
...AND YOU'RE OFF THE HOOK.

WHAT IF I DON'T GIVE HIM VERY MUCH DATA?

THEN YOU'LL HAVE TO PAY THE FULL PRICE-- IN CASH.
No more payment plans.

A gadget? Emotions?

IF YOU CAN'T PAY...
CASH

KA-THOOM
HSST
I'M SCARED. DID HE JUST SUMMON SOME-THING!?
THERE'S NO TELLING WHAT THIS COMPANY MIGHT DO...
KA-THOOM

Johnny Rock
SHOTBAR
I'LL SEE YA LATER!
SO I ENDED UP ACCEPTING THE DEAL!
WELL, AT LEAST I WON'T HAVE TO PAY A MILLION DOLLARS.
...
I CAN STAY WITH YOU AWHILE LONGER.
THAT MAKES ME HAPPY.
I'M SO HAPPY!
HUH? ABOUT WHAT?

HEY, YOU FELT HAPPY JUST NOW.
HE'S EVEN BLUSHING.
How sweet.
TEACH ME EVERYTHING...
WHAT !?
WOW, IT TURNED RED! IT WORKS!
...ABOUT GIRLS. ABOUT YOU.
GASP
BA-BUMP
BA-BUMP
BA-BUMP
BA-BUMP
This is embarrassing ...

SOSHI!!
?
...

UH...
UM...
FWISH
HUH?

WUP

IT'S BLACK ...

ACK

WHAT !?

WHO WAS THAT?

HE'S NOBODY!

THAT RING IS DEFECTIVE!!

...

WHAM

YOU'RE HOME LATE.

I WAS LOOKING FOR A JOB.
Yeah.
Yeah?
HEY, MAKE ME SOME DINNER! I'M HUNGRY!

CAN'T YOU MAKE YOUR OWN DINNER SOMETIMES!?
I CAN'T COOK, AND YOUR FOOD TASTES JUST LIKE MOM'S. ARE YOU IN A BAD MOOD OR SOMETHING?

IT'S NOTHING.
Oh.
GUESS WHAT? DAD CALLED.
HE'S IN THE MIDDLE EAST.

THE MIDDLE EAST!? HE'S GONNA GET HIMSELF KILLED...
HE'S A FAMOUS PHOTOGRAPHER! IT'S HIS JOB TO GALLIVANT ALL OVER THE GLOBE!

HE'S PROBABLY GOT TEN WOMEN IN EVERY COUNTRY.
YOU KNOW, SOSHI...
Edmunds Columbine

...WE HAVE PLENTY OF MONEY. WHY GET A JOB? JUST FIND A GIRLFRIEND AND RELIEVE YOUR FRUSTRATIONS!
The pent-up ones.
SHUT UP!
I'M NOT FRUSTRATED!

HOW'S IT GOING WITH RIIKO?
KRUNCH
EGG
THERE'S NOTHING BETWEEN US.
GLUP
I THINK SHE'S GOT A BOY-FRIEND.
WHAT!?
THAT'S IMPOS-SIBLE!!
I'VE KNOWN HER FOR YEARS! SHE'LL ***NEVER*** GET A GUY!
SAY THAT TO HER FACE, AND SHE'LL KICK YOUR BUTT.
BUT SHE ALREADY HAS YOU!
!

Now, the title... I had trouble with this one, too. At first, the working title was *Lover Shop*, but that was only going to apply to the first episode, so it wasn't right. I needed something bold, yet something that hinted at the content. I had nothing! I agonized for days, putting words together. The deadline was looming, so I was randomly going through my electronic English dictionary, and I came across the word "absolute." I was reminded of the term "absolute pitch." What if I tacked on the word "boyfriend" instead? Night is supposed to be the perfect boyfriend. Actually, the title didn't have to be limited to Night--it could refer to any boyfriend for Riiko...

My editor at the time wasn't quite convinced, but I pressed for it. Actually, I couldn't think of anything else. Besides, my assistants and friends liked it, too. It turned out to be popular with readers. Thank goodness. ♪ And it was easy to remember, so it all turned out well in the end.

Coming up with titles is really hard. They have to have panache, but they can't sound too much like your previous work or anyone else's. I can name one-shot comics without much thought, but that won't do for longer series! You have to develop a big vocabulary. We discussed a lot of titles that we thought were brilliant during the preliminary meeting. ♪

Titles of movies and anime and stuff. They all must've gone through the same agony. You don't want people to think you couldn't come up with anything good. ♪ Long wordy titles aren't so good, although some of them may be intentional. Maybe they sound more literary. In any case, it's a challenge to make a title stick in people's memories.

WHAT ARE YOU SAYING?

OH!

I KNOW!! INVITE HER OVER FOR DINNER!!

SHHHHHH

WHAT'S WITH SOSHI? HE DIDN'T MAKE A WISECRACK LIKE HE USUALLY DOES.

NOW NIGHT THINKS THERE'S SOME-THING BETWEEN US!

BEE-BEE-BEEP

CHAK

RIIKO, THE PHONE'S RINGING.

AAAAAH!!

NO, I HAVEN'T EATEN YET...

OKAY, I'LL BE OVER IN A FEW.

IT MIGHT BE A BIT AWKWARD, BUT MASAKI WILL BE THERE, TOO.
ARE YOU GOING SOME-WHERE, RIIKO?
BEEP
OVER TO SOSHI'S ...
HMPH
I MEAN, NEXT DOOR!
YOU'LL HAVE TO STAY HERE, NIGHT!
WE HAVE TO KEEP THE FACT THAT WE'RE LIVING TOGETHER A SECRET!!
NOD
...
WHAT WERE YOU THINKING?
AW, YOU KNOW YOU'RE THRILLED TO BE COOKING FOR THREE!
WAIT, WHY DID YOU CHANGE CLOTHES ?
DING DONG
THERE SHE IS!

HI THERE.
COME IN!
Hey! YOU SMELL NICE. FRESH OUT OF THE SHOWER?

I FORGOT I WAS MEETING MY GIRLFRIEND!
MAKE YOURSELF AT HOME!
!!
WHAT !?

WHAM

NO !!

I'LL GET YOU, MASAKI ...
Uh-oh.

IS SOSHI MAD?
WHAT'S HIS PROBLEM ?

MAYBE I SHOULD GO HOME...
HAVE A SEAT.
THERE'S NO USE LETTING THE FOOD GO TO WASTE.
IN FACT, EAT MASAKI'S SHARE, TOO.
MEAN-WHILE...
ISN'T RIIKO EVER COMING HOME?
FWIP FWIP
IT'S ONLY BEEN FIVE MINUTES.
...

THIS IS GOOD!

OH.

HOW LONG AGO DID YOUR MOM DIE, SOSHI?

THREE YEARS.

IF YOU HAVE SOMETHING TO SAY, SPIT IT OUT!

KLINK

NOW WHAT!?

She started it.

YOU'RE MORE FICKLE THAN I THOUGHT, IS ALL.

HUH?

YOU SEEMED ALL BROKEN UP ABOUT ISHIZEKI...

BUT YOU'VE ALREADY FOUND ANOTHER GUY, I SEE.

THAT WAS A QUICK RECOVERY, BUT I CAN SEE WHY. HE'S REALLY GOOD-LOOKING.
!!
WELL, YOU'VE FINALLY GOT A BOYFRIEND. GOOD FOR YOU.
Um...
SOSHI, HE'S ACTUALLY A MAIL ORDER...
MAIL ORDER?

OH!

"LET ME MAKE SURE YOU UNDER-STAND."

"YOU'LL ALSO HAVE TO PAY IF ANYONE FINDS OUT NIGHT ISN'T HUMAN."

MAIL ORDER WHAT !?
SHUT UP, FOUR-EYES !!
GRARR
ARE YOU CRAZY !?
SO WHAT IF I'VE GOT A BOY-FRIEND!?
GRR
IT'S NONE OF YOUR BUSI-NESS!!
New orlins Los, C. INC. such as

...
WHAP
I'M GOING HOME! THANKS FOR DINNER!

I'LL PUT THE DISHES AWAY!
KLINK
DON'T BOTHER!
GIVE ME THAT!
I'LL DO IT! LET GO!
KREESH
OW!
OUCH ...

ARE YOU OKAY!? I'M SORRY ...
I'M ALL RIGHT.

STAY PUT. LET ME SEE THAT.
GULP

UM.
NO, IT'S NOTHING! I'M FINE!
WHUP
IT'S JUST A SCRATCH ...
THROB
!!

shopping by recaus
UM ...
Er...
SORRY ...
...
BA-BUMP
BA-BUMP
BA-BUMP
HUH ?
WHY HAS SOSHI GONE QUIET AGAIN?
AND WHY IS MY HEART BEATING SO FAST !?
BA-BUMP

KRASH
!?
RIIKO!

NIGHT!?
How'd he get on the balcony !?
WHOA!
...
SHOOM
WHAT ARE YOU DOING ...
...TO MY GIRL !?
KA-POW

RIIKO, ARE YOU ALL RIGHT !?
UM, SOSHI'S THE ONE WHO GOT HIT!
NIGHT, WHAT ARE YOU ...!?

I HEARD YOU SHOUT SO I CAME TO CHECK ON YOU, AND I SAW *HIM*!
NO, NO!! SOSHI'S JUST A FRIEND !!

SCHOOL ...
I'M SORRY, SOSHI! ARE YOU OKAY!?
Y-YEAH ...

A FRIEND ?
YES!! WE'VE GONE TO THE SAME SCHOOL SINCE WE WERE LITTLE. ANYWAY, THERE'S NOTHING GOING ON!
I'M GONNA TAKE HIM HOME NOW!! I'M SO SORRY!!

WHAM
STAGGER
WHAT A PUNCH...
THIS IS TEMPERED GLASS.
AND THIS IS THE FOURTH FLOOR. HOW DID HE...?
WHAT...
...IS HE?
YOU CAN'T DO THAT SORT OF THING, NIGHT!!
IT'S SWEET THAT YOU WANT TO PROTECT ME, BUT...
...

HE SAVED ME FROM THE MOMENT, THOUGH.
Poor Soshi.
IT WAS GETTING KINDA AWKWARD...
RIIKO...
I...
...WANT TO GO TO SCHOOL, TOO!
HUH !?
I WANT TO BE JUST LIKE THAT FRIEND OF YOURS.
BUT YOU CAN'T GO TO SCHOOL...
THAT'S A SWELL IDEA!
SPOP
WHAT ARE YOU DOING THERE!?
With a lolly-pop!?

THERE'D BE LOTS OF GIRLS AT SCHOOL.
NIGHT COULD GATHER A LOT MORE DATA THERE!
I'LL GET THE COMPANY TO SET IT UP.
BUT FIRST, GIVE ME ALL THE MONEY YOU'VE GOT!
WHAT KIND OF COMPANY IS THIS!?
TAKE NIGHT TO SCHOOL? CAN I DO THAT?
Yes!
ESPECIALLY AFTER WHAT HAPPENED WITH SOSHI.
A BAD FEELING.
WHOA!! WHAT DID YOU AND RIIKO DO!?
NOTHING!
DARN IT. WHY ME !?

Absolute Boyfriend

SCHOOL
Act 6
Let's Go to
School!

TWEET
HERE'S MY UNIFORM!!
I'M GOING TO RIIKO'S SCHOOL TODAY!!
TA-DAH
Yippee!
FROM NOW ON, YOUR NAME'S NIGHT TENJO!
TENJO? AS IN "HEAVENLY CASTLE"?*
WHAT ARE YOU DOING HERE, ANYWAY?

*The meaning of Night's last name in Japanese

THAT'S HIS LAST NAME! THE COMPANY IS KRONOS *HEAVEN*. GET IT?
THAT'S NOT VERY CREATIVE.
Look who's talking.
BUT WHY ARE YOU HAVING BREAKFAST WITH US!?
LISTEN, YOUR SCHOOL'S A GREAT PLACE FOR NIGHT TO COLLECT DATA, BUT IF ANYONE FINDS OUT HE'S AN ANDROID...
I KNOW! I HAVE TO PAY YOU A MILLION IN CASH!
LIKE I'D TELL ANYONE ...
...THAT I BOUGHT AN ARTIFICIAL LOVER. HOW EMBARRAS-SING!!
C'MON, RIIKO! HURRY!
YAY YAY
He's like a first grader.
I'M SORRY, BUT WE HAVE TO GO TO SCHOOL SEPARATELY!
WE DON'T WANT ANYONE TO SUSPECT THAT WE'RE LIVING TOGETHER.

I'M FINE WITH THAT.

I'LL ENDURE ANYTHING TO BE WITH RIIKO!

SOB

HOW NOBLE ...

DON'T YOU HAVE TO GO TO WORK?

I FEEL A LITTLE GUILTY. I'M SORRY, NIGHT...

CHAK

I'D BETTER GET GOING, TOO.

OOPS...

HI... THERE ...

HEY.

SINCE DINNER THE OTHER DAY...
...IT'S BEEN WEIRD BETWEEN SOSHI AND ME...
NEXT STOP, SEIBA HIGH SCHOOL ...

SKREECH
!!

Um...
SORRY!
IT'S OKAY.

MURMUR MURMUR
?

HI, MIKA! WHAT'S GOING ON?
Hey.
HI, RIIKO. HI, SOSHI.

THERE'S A GUY ON TOP OF THE SCHOOL GATE!
RIIKO
HEY!
Oh. RIIKO!
NIGHT!! GET DOWN!!
THAT'S THE GUY ...
!

TUP

WOW!
TUMP
Whoa!
THAT WAS AWESOME!!
JABBER JABBER

AAGH
HE'S MAKING A SCENE ALREADY!!
THIS IS MY FIRST DAY! I WAS SO EXCITED, I WANTED TO DRINK IN THE VIEW!
WHO ASKED YOU?
DID YOU TRANSFER HERE?

YEAH.
NICE TO MEET YOU, SOSHI.
UH... NICE...
...TO MEET YOU.
You punched me.

GASP
GLANCE
FWIP
SEE YOU LATER!
Excuse me.
HOW DO I GET TO THE ADMINISTRATION OFFICE?
OH... IT'S JUST UP THOSE STAIRS!
PAT
HE'S CUTE!
HE MUST BE NEW!!
Huh?
IT'S RED, FOR HAPPINESS.

Mumble
WHY'S HE IGNORING YOU?
ISN'T HE YOUR BOYFRIEND?
ACK
WHAT WAS THAT?

NO!! HE'S... UH...
...JUST SOMEONE MY DAD KNOWS!! HE'S BEEN OVERSEAS!!

"WHAT ARE YOU DOING TO MY GIRLFRIEND!?"
YOU DON'T HAVE TO HIDE IT.

IT'S NONE OF MY BUSINESS.
C'mon!
RIIKO, TELL ME!
...

Hey.
ISHIZEKI, DID YOU SEE THAT?
ISN'T THAT THE GUY WHO PUNCHED YOU!?
!!

Ahem...
WE HAVE A NEW TRANSFER STUDENT.
I'M NIGHT TENJO. NICE TO MEET YOU!
GRIN
GRIN
Um...
HE'S BEEN ABROAD... ON FAMILY BUSINESS.
MADE THAT UP.
RIIKO, IT'S HIM!
OH YEAH, GAKU SAID HE'D PUT NIGHT IN MY CLASS...
What kind of company does he work for?
Wow!
HE LOOKS COOL.
Wow!
THE GIRLS LIKE HIM!!
LIKE A MODEL!
He's so tall!

KLAK
BLUSH
I FEEL SO PROUD!
Girls, face forward!
AND SOSHI LOOKS REALLY MAD.
...

Hey!
NIGHT, WHERE WERE YOU LIVING ABROAD ?
LOTS OF PLACES! THE U.S., SPAIN, FRANCE...
...
UH-OH

AFRICA, NEW ZEALAND, INDIA, RUSSIA, ANTARCTICA ...
THAT'S ALL OVER THE WORLD !!

FOR REAL!? WOW!
Not → very believable.
CAN YOU SPEAK FRENCH? SAY SOME-THING!

JE M'APPELLE NIGHT. JE SUIS ETUDIANT. IL ME FAIT TRÈS HEUREUX AUJOURD'HUI PARCE QUE JE SUIS ICI AVEC MA PETITE AMIE. LE CHIEN EST TRÈS GROS...
HE REALLY CAN!!
WOW !!
Gee.
THAT'S AMAZING!

WAS MULTI-LINGUAL ONE OF MY OPTIONS ?
I can't remember anymore ...
HE'S INCRED-IBLE.

YAY
YAY
OH YEAH, I HAVE TO GATHER DATA.

FWISH
DO YOU WANT ME TO SPEAK ANOTHER LANGUAGE ...
... JUST FOR YOU?
PUFF
BOOOM
YEAH !!
Say any-thing !!
WOW, HOT-PINK, PLEA-SURE!

WELL, I WAS THE ONE WHO TOLD HIM TO KEEP OUR RELATION-SHIP A SECRET...
GLANCE
!
KRAK KRAK
I GET IT, HE'S COLLECTING DATA FROM THOSE GIRLS!
Uh-oh
SAY SOME-THING IN ANTARC-TICAN!
FWUMP
SPEAK AMAZON-IAN!!
There's no such thing.
...BUT THIS REALLY SUCKS.
?
Hmph
Hey.
WHERE'S THE COOL NEW FRESH-MAN?
Over there!
OH MY GOSH, HE'S GOR-GEOUS!
THE TRANSFER APPLICA-TION'S REALLY HARD!
He must be smart!

Look.
HE'S ALREADY A CELEBRITY, EVEN WITH THE OLDER GIRLS!
HMPH, IT'S NOT HARD TO SEE WHY.
Lucky guy.
RIGHT, SOSHI?
...
OOH!
ALWAYS EAGER TO PLEASE.
?
BONK
HEY.
Psst.
AREN'T YOU RIIKO'S BOY-FRIEND?
!
STOP FLIRTING WITH OTHER GIRLS.

OF COURSE, I'M HER ...
"DON'T TELL ANY-ONE!"
... MURFLE FLERGEN!
MURFLE FLERGEN?
I'M JUST GATHER-ING DATA!
DATA!?
FWEEET
GATHER AROUND, PEOPLE!!
GASP
A BAR CODE!?
What's wrong?
We'll split into two teams ...
IS NIGHT DOING OKAY?
STARING AT NIGHT AGAIN? GOT A THING FOR HIM?
SHALL WE HOLD A STRATEGY SESSION?
OH, C'MON, MIKA!!

POW
FWASH

Now then...volume 1 is almost finished! I hope to be able to include character data and other extras in the next volume. I'm working on this and *Fushigi Yûgi: Genbu Kaiden* at the same time. It's going to be pretty tough until I get used to the workload. Volume 1 of *FY:GK* is coming out at the same time as volume 1 of *Absolute Boyfriend*. Please check it out, too! You don't even need to be familiar with the previous *FY* titles. And I have other stuff going on, as well (smile). If you're curious, check out my friend's homepage:

http://homepage2.nifty.com/nankou/
(The site is called "Warau Choro no Seikatsu" or "Laughing Old Man's Life.")

And let the Shojo Beat team know what you think of *Absolute Boyfriend*!

Absolute Boyfriend
c/o Shojo Beat
VIZ Media, LLC
P.O. Box 77010
San Francisco CA 94107

Oh, and please don't include any postage or self-addressed envelopes. I'd really like to write replies, but I don't have time. I'm sorry.

Oh! Maybe I could write replies in these columns! I could withhold the names, like on radio talk shows. There are a lot of individual readers I think about. I'm always mumbling to myself when I'm reading my fan mail (smile). I really wish I could reply directly. Sigh... but there's just no time!! I'll have to learn to take power naps! I always end up sleeping for ten hours! Without an alarm clock, that is. They say people who sleep three to four or nine to ten hours a night have shorter life spans. Seven to eight hours' sleep is ideal. Whatever. (What am I saying?) I gotta try harder. See you in volume 2!!

I hope winter comes soon.

--Yuu Watase and the Shojo Beat team.

AND THERE'S A BAR CODE BEHIND HIS EAR. A TATTOO, I GUESS.

A BAR CODE!?

AND HE SAID HE FLIRTS WITH ALL THE GIRLS TO GET DATA.

ARE YOU TWO REALLY...

UH-OH!!

I'M GETTING NERVOUS!

SHOOM

SORRY, I GOTTA PEE!

Hey.

WAIT!

TMP
HUH?
THERE'S NOBODY HERE.
Did I miss him?
TUP
EEEK!!

SWUP
GOTCHA. ♬
NIGHT !?
YOU'RE STILL THE ONLY ONE FOR ME, RIIKO...
BA-BUMP
HUH? WHAT?
BA-BUMP
BA-BUMP
GAKU TOLD ME TO GET DATA FROM OTHER GIRLS...
...BUT I'D RATHER SPEND TIME WITH YOU... LIKE THIS.
BA-BUMP
BA-BUMP
BA-BUMP
...

I'm...
I'M GLAD YOU DIDN'T GET ANY DATA FROM ME!
AW!
THE RING WOULD'VE BEEN BLUE FOR ANGER.
BECAUSE I WAS A LITTLE JEALOUS.
I can't tell him-- it's too embarrassing!
RIIKO...
GASP
DOES IT FEEL GOOD WHEN I DO THIS?

HEH
IT'S PINK, FOR PLEA-SURE.
H-HEY, NIGHT!
WE CAN'T DO THIS HERE!
OH, LOOK.
BLUSH
IT'S GONNA TURN BLUE IN A SECOND!
YEAH, BUT IT'S STILL PINK.
RIIKO!
KLAK
HAVING FUN !?
YOU BOUNCE BACK PRETTY QUICK.

YOU MAKE ME SICK!!
I-ISHIZEKI !?

DOOOOOM
WOOOOO
AND YOU... YOU'RE TENJO, RIGHT?
YOU MADE ME LOOK BAD BEFORE.
NOW IT'S YOUR TURN TO EAT HUMBLE PIE!
HE LOOKS LIKE A WIMP. C'MERE!
SHWAK

HUH?
KRAK
WHA --?
WHAM
THWAK

THUD
KRK
YOU ...
I WARNED YOU NOT TO BOTHER MY GIRL-FRIEND!!
SHAKE SHAKE SHAKE
WAIT!
WHAK
S-STOP!
!?
BRAM
KRAK
STAY AWAY FROM HER!
TH UD
HE'S FAST !!
AND SHE'S NOT A SLUT!!

SHE'S ...
!
DAMN!
SHOOM
...THE BEST GIRL-FRIEND IN THE WORLD!
THANK YOU, NIGHT, BUT I'M NOT WORTHY ...
I'M REALLY NOT SO GREAT.
KLAK

THAT ...
SUCKED.
Huh?
YOU SAW?
YOU SAW WHAT THEY DID!?
I WAS TALKING ABOUT *YOU*!
HUH?
YOU'RE PATHETIC!

BUT ...
IT WAS RIIKO'S FAULT!!
YOU WERE RIGHT ABOUT HER!

YOU WARNED ME THAT SHE WAS GOING TO ASK ME OUT ...
YOU SAID SHE USES GUYS LIKE TISSUES, THEN SHE COMES WHINING TO YOU FOR ADVICE AND MONEY!

YOU WERE RIGHT. SHE'S ALREADY WITH SOMEONE ELSE!

THEN NIGHT REALLY IS RIIKO'S BOY-FRIEND?

DUH!! JUST LOOK WHAT HE DID TO ME!!

MIKA!

I'M ONLY INTERESTED ...

...IN GUYS WHO BELONG TO OTHER GIRLS.

To be continued in volume 2!

Yuu Watase

Birthday: March 5 (Pisces)

Blood type: B

Born and raised in Osaka.

Hobbies: listening to music, reading. Likes most music besides *enka* (traditional Japanese ballads) and heavy metal. Lately into health and wellness, like massage, mineral waters and wheat grass juice. But her job is her biggest "hobby"!

Debut title: *Pajama de Ojama* (An intrusion in Pajamas) (*Shojo Comics*, 1989, No. 3)

See her current stuff in *Shojo Beat* magazine!

ABSOLUTE BOYFRiEND

Vol. 1

The Shojo Beat Manga Edition

This graphic novel contains material that was originally published in English in *Shojo Beat* magazine, January-December 2006 issues.

STORY AND ART BY
YUU WATASE

English Adaptation/Lance Caselman
Translation/Lillian Olsen
Touch-up Art & Lettering/Freeman Wong
Design/Courtney Utt
Editor/Yuki Takagaki

Managing Editor/Megan Bates
Editorial Director/Elizabeth Kawasaki
VP & Editor in Chief/Yumi Hoashi
Sr. Director of Acquisitions/Rika Inouye
Sr. VP of Marketing/Liza Coppola
Exec. VP of Sales & Marketing/John Easum
Publisher/Hyoe Narita

Printed in Canada

Published by ViZ Media, LLC
P.O. Box 77010
San Francisco, CA 94107

Shojo Beat Manga Edition
10 9 8 7 6 5 4
First printing, January 2006
Second printing, March 2006
Third printing, August 2006
Fourth printing, September 2006

www.viz.com

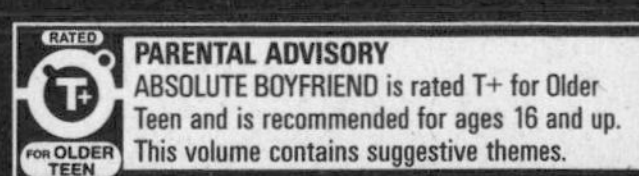

store.viz.com

Thank you for reading the *Absolute Boyfriend,* Volume 1 manga. Please turn to the back and enjoy a special excerpt of the *Kamikaze Girls* novel, written by Novala Takemoto.

"Hey girlie, my name's Shirayuri. Would Miz Momoko be around at home?"

If that was an attempt at polite language, it was a shambles. But anyway, being the "girlie" addressed, I said yes. Oh dear, this was that Ichiko Shirayuri who really wanted Versace no matter what! From the clumsy style of her letter I had assumed she would be about thirteen years old, but there was no question now that she was a bona-fide high-schooler, about the same age as I. It would seem the awkwardness of her letter derived not from childishness but from simple ignorance, or should I say, stupidity. As I fidgeted in the garden, thinking what a pain it was to get involved with someone of this sort, the *sukeban* spoke again.

"So could you conduct me over to Miz Momoko if you will?"

To this, I answered nervously, "Um, I'm Momoko, actually."

You should have seen her face when she heard that. She twisted her mouth and widened her eyes, and her expression could have been taken as wanting to pick a fight, or being really sad and about to burst into tears, either way. TO BE CONTINUED...

something sporting so many decorations both in front and back actually run? Just the accessories alone look pretty heavy—is what I thought as I gazed upon the chopper from a distance, giving it minus a thousand style points for the garish bad taste of its color scheme and utterly nonexistent sense of design. I mean to say, an ordinary motorcycle would probably be fine with all those embellishments so long as it had enough horsepower, but the bike in front of my eyes was, in spite of all the gnarly remodeling, a scooter. No matter how you looked at it, it was a plain old 50cc scooter.

This freakish scooter stopped blasting its horn when it realized I was there. And then, the person who had been doing the blasting, namely the person who had been riding the bike, got off of it and started walking toward me. The person had straight bleached-blond hair down to her shoulders, wore blue eye shadow and bright red lipstick, and had on a navy-blue school uniform comprised of a short jacket and a very long skirt with a prodigious number of pleats, which dragged on the ground. On her feet were—well, it would sound good to call them "mules," but actually they were cheap purple slip-on sandals of the type moms wear when going out to the neighborhood supermarket, and their sparkles glinted in the sun. *Wow, a* sukeban, *and a super old-school one too... Who knew bad girls wearing outfits like this still existed? Hand it to Ibaraki—this place is deep. If a curator for a natural history museum saw her, she'd immediately be captured and exhibited next to a stegosaur skeleton in the Fossils section.* As I was thinking this and watching her approach with some trepidation because, let's face it, people like that are kinda scary, the *sukeban* yelled out to me in a loud voice.

heard the noisy cacophony of an engine, probably from the motorcycle of a passing Yanki. The loud vrooming sound gradually got louder, and then it stopped. Just when I thought it was finally quiet again, the earsplitting sound of those horns that Yanki like to put on their bikes and cars, arranged to play the *Godfather* theme, rang out: *parara rararara rarararaa*!! *parara rararara rararararaa*!!!! It was blasted out repeatedly, over and over. The source of the sound seemed to be right in front of our house, or at least very close to it, so I ventured out into the yard. The most outrageous motorcycle was parked out front.

In front of the handlebars towered an indescribably strange sunshade-type thing, fixed willy-nilly without any thought of balance, and painted with the Rising Sun. The seat had a backrest, which stretched so high skyward that if Giant Baba stood behind it, his head probably wouldn't show over the top. The seat itself was leopard-print. And the sunshade and backrest were not the only elongated features: behind the backrest were attached what would be called "tail fins" on a car, I believe, like super-long fake nails only a thousand times larger, and these too spread upward, reaching about as high as the seat and painted a camouflage pattern. The muffler was twisted, turned out, and extended, and again, pointed up. This muffler, while oddly shaped, was an ordinary metallic silver color, but the rest of the body was painted shocking pink all over, and overlaid with glitter. This was obviously a hot rod belonging to a Yanki, or more specifically, a Zokki—a member of a Bosozoku biker gang. I had seen bikes of this sort in Amagasaki and here in Ibaraki, but this was my first experience of seeing one this crazily souped-up from right up close. *Could* of which was that she lived in Shimotsuma too, so would it be all right if she came by sometime to see the merchandise for herself? Well, if she was just a middle schooler, I didn't see any problem with inviting her to the house. I called the cell phone number given in her letter and arranged to have her come over after lunch that Saturday.

School ended at noon on Saturday, and I went straight home because that girl was coming over. Even though she was younger than me, it would be our first meeting and moreover, she was going to be buying clothes from me. Thinking it would be rude to greet her without being dressed at least somewhat properly, I decided to wear my white rose-patterned lace blouse with a black velvet knee-length skirt that's decorated in front with ladder lace and all kinds of other white lace, while the back is like curtains that are closed at the top and draped back at the sides, and where the velvet would ordinarily fall—namely the middle of the hips—layers of tulle peek out like bustles. On my head I perched a large white ribbon made to be worn like a headdress, and then I went to the room where all the bogus Versace was stored to arrange everything, sorting it into piles by type while I waited.

We had agreed to meet at one thirty, but she didn't appear. Maybe she was lost? Perhaps my directions had been inadequate. I'd told her to go just a little bit east on Route 131 where it intersects Route 249, and take the first left, which is a narrow road—it was an ordinary farmhouse with rice paddies in front, and she'd see it right after she turned. Maybe that wasn't detailed enough? But there was nothing around the house, so how else could I explain how to get here? As I sat there waiting, I suddenly

Kamikaze Girls *depicts the unusual friendship between a bored girl stuck in rural Japan who fantasizes about 18th century France and a spunky biker girl. Please enjoy this excerpt from the novel that inspired the manga and popular movie, both available from VIZ Media.*

In the end, I decided to contact only the girl from Ibaraki, who happened to live in Shimotsuma too and was named Ichiko Shirayuri. "Miz Ryugasaki. Pleeze let me buy your Versace stuff. I don't have much money so I can't pay you a whole lot, but I really want some Versace no matter what, so I beg you wherefore pleeze." The writing was printed out in block letters, *please* was spelled "pleeze," and the ending had the mysterious, nonsensical clause, "so I beg you wherefore pleeze." I suppose she meant "so I beg you therefore please," which *still* wouldn't make much sense. But how was I to answer a request couched in the interrogative form of "wherefore please"? Guessing that the writer was maybe in the first year of middle school, I sent her the following answer: "Dear Miss Shirayuri, Thank you for your letter. Regarding the merchandise, I have a considerable variety of items in large quantities. If you would kindly inform me what sort of things you desire, I will select suitable items and send you another letter detailing their color, design, shape, and other particulars. As for the price, I am open to negotiation. However, as I stated in my ad, all of the Versace items I have are counterfeits, and I request your understanding of this point." Wondering if I had used too many big words and complicated sentence structures—did she even know what "particulars" and "negotiation" meant?— I sent off the letter anyway. I received an answer right away, the gist

Kamikaze Girls

Novala Takemoto

Translated by
Akemi Wegmüller

WELCOME TO THE EXCITING NEW WORLD OF VIZ MEDIA FICTION!

What you hold in your hands is a sneak preview of a bold step in publishing: America's No.1 manga publisher, VIZ Media, is proud to debut its fiction line, featuring the very best in new writing from Japan!

Our debut titles include *Fullmetal Alchemist: Land of Sand*, a spin-off based on the smash-success manga and anime; *Socrates in Love*, a stirring love story and the all-time best-selling novel in Japan; and *Ghost in the Shell 2: Innocence, After the Long Goodbye*, a powerful vision of the future set in the world of Mamoru Oshii's hit anime film.

Forthcoming titles include *Steamboy*, a novelization of the latest epic from anime auteur, Katsuhiro Otomo (director of *Akira*), and *Kamikaze Girls*, the Japanese cult classic exploring Japan's outré "Goth Lolita" subculture.

In 2004, VIZ released its first foray into fiction, the surprise best seller, *Battle Royale*, which demonstrated that there was a hungry audience for new fiction from Japan.

Now with the *Shojo Beat* fiction imprint, we hope you'll discover that when it comes to the exploding universe of Japanese pop culture, manga is just the beginning!

Will a musical fairy and a magical violin be enough to help Kahoko compete against five hot and talented boys?

La Corda d'Oro™

by Yuki Kure

In stores October 3, 2006!

Only $8.99

Shojo Beat™ MANGA from the HEART

THE REAL DRAMA BEGINS IN...

On sale at:
www.shojobeat.com

Also available at your local bookstore and comic store.